Snapchat Traffic Booster

Snapchat Traffic Booster

Erin Frenchie

First Printing, 2024

ISBN/SKU: 979-8-3303-6850-1

EISBN: 979-8-3303-6851-8

CONTENTS

Introduction

To secure long-term success and remain relevant in an ever-evolving business landscape, it is crucial to continuously adapt to new trends and technologies. Staying ahead in social media is particularly important, and integrating emerging platforms such as Snapchat into your strategy is a forward-thinking approach that can position your brand advantageously for the future.

Snapchat: Embracing the Next Generation

One of the most compelling reasons to engage with Snapchat is its significant traction among younger demographics. Specifically, the platform has become a favorite among individuals aged 12 to 24. This age group not only represents the current younger generation of consumers but also the future market. By establishing a presence on Snapchat early, your brand can build connections with these young, influential consumers before they become major purchasing powerhouses. This proactive approach ensures that your brand is well-positioned to engage with them as they transition into significant buying roles.

Creating Engagement and Excitement

Snapchat is renowned for its unique and interactive features that set it apart from other social media platforms. The platform's design encourages creativity and spontaneous interaction, offering users a dynamic and engaging experience. Brands that leverage Snapchat can tap into this excitement by providing exclusive content, such as behind-the-scenes looks at events or products, special promotions, and limited-time discounts or giveaways. The fleeting nature of Snapchat's content—where posts disappear after a set period—creates a sense of urgency and anticipation, enhancing user engagement and making each interaction feel special and unique.

Enhancing Your Online Presence

Integrating Snapchat into your social media strategy can significantly boost your online visibility. Although you may already have established profiles on platforms like Twitter, Facebook, and Pinterest, expanding your presence to include Snapchat offers new opportunities for growth. This addition not only helps you reach new audiences but also reinforces your connection with existing followers across different platforms. By promoting your Snapchat profile through your other social media channels, you can drive traffic and attract followers from these networks to Snapchat, further broadening your overall reach.

Given Snapchat's impressive growth trajectory, with 200 million active users each month, it is evident that the platform is a key player in the future of social media. To stay ahead of the curve and effectively prepare for the next generation of consumers, it is essential to embrace Snapchat and integrate it into your broader social media strategy. By doing so, you position your brand to capture the attention of tomorrow's buyers and enhance your business's growth and success.

1

What is Snapchat?

Snapchat has emerged as a remarkably influential social media platform, capturing significant attention and popularity in recent times. Major brands are increasingly establishing their presence on Snapchat, not only by creating profiles but also by utilizing the platform's discovery system for advertising. While Snapchat shares the fundamental concept of creating a profile and attracting followers with other social media platforms, it distinguishes itself with unique methods of communication and information sharing.

Understanding How Snapchat Works

Snapchat operates with a distinctive approach to media communication, focusing primarily on images and videos rather than text. Unlike traditional social media platforms such as Twitter or Facebook, which rely heavily on textual content, Snapchat's interactions are predominantly visual. Users share photos and videos, and the content is designed to be ephemeral, lasting only from 1 to 10 seconds before disappearing. This fleeting nature of posts is a key feature that sets Snapchat apart, creating a sense of immediacy and urgency for its users.

If you are unfamiliar with Snapchat, envision a scenario where you receive a notification about a new post from someone you follow. When you visit their profile, you encounter a brief video or a photo with a caption. If you don't view the content quickly, it vanishes, reflecting Snapchat's unique approach to content sharing. This dynamic interaction fosters a more engaging and spontaneous form of communication, differentiating Snapchat from other social media networks.

The Significance of Snapchat

Snapchat is poised to play a leading role in the future of social media. Its appeal to younger audiences, particularly teenagers, underscores its potential to shape the next generation of digital communication. This potential has not gone unnoticed; even Facebook recognized Snapchat's value and made a substantial $3 billion acquisition offer, which Snapchat's founders declined, believing in the platform's future success. This bold move highlights the confidence in Snapchat's unique position in the social media landscape.

The essence of Snapchat lies in its ability to facilitate social interaction, build followings, and foster connections based on shared interests and emotional engagement. It represents a shift toward a future where visual content may overshadow traditional text-based posts. Esteemed brands such as Mashable, National Geographic, and Comedy Central have already embraced Snapchat for advertising, demonstrating the platform's growing influence and potential. For businesses aiming to remain relevant and connect with a younger audience, Snapchat is not just an option but a necessity.

2

Getting Your Brand on Snapchat

To fully leverage the benefits of Snapchat for your brand, the first step is to establish a presence on the platform. This chapter will guide you through the process of creating a Snapchat account and optimizing your profile to effectively engage with your audience and enhance your marketing efforts.

Getting Started with Snapchat

The initial step is to download the Snapchat application, available for both Android and iOS devices. Unfortunately, Snapchat does not support Windows or less common operating systems at this time. Once you have installed the app on your mobile device, open it to find the options to either sign in or sign up.

Creating Your Account

To sign up, you will need to provide several key pieces of information:

- **Email Address:** Choose an email address that you regularly check, ideally your primary business email. This is crucial as it will be used for account verification and important communications. Avoid using a temporary or rarely checked email address to ensure you do not miss critical updates.

- **Password and Date of Birth:** Set a secure password and enter your date of birth using the date picker tool provided by most mobile devices. There are generally no stringent restrictions for creating a password, but ensure it is strong to protect your account.

- **Phone Number:** Enter a valid mobile number where you can receive a verification code. This step is necessary to complete the sign-up process and fully activate your account.

- **Verification Code:** After entering your phone number, you will receive a verification code via SMS. Navigate to the appropriate section in the app to input this code, which is typically found under the gear icon that accesses the settings menu. Further navigation details will be discussed in Chapter Four.

Customizing Your Profile

Unlike other social media platforms such as Twitter or Facebook, Snapchat does not offer a traditional profile setup or logo upload option directly through the app. Instead, you can only customize your profile picture by taking a photo or using an existing image. Snapchat's method of capturing multiple quick successive images can make it challenging to obtain a high-quality, professional-looking profile picture, which may not be ideal for brands.

For a more polished and professional profile, there are alternative methods to digitally insert your logo. Detailed instructions on achieving this high-quality setup will be provided in Chapter Four.

3

How to Use Snapchat?

Now that you have successfully signed up for Snapchat and established your brand on the platform, it's essential to familiarize yourself with how to navigate and utilize the app effectively. This chapter will provide a foundational overview, covering the basic functions and navigation techniques necessary to get started. Future chapters will delve into more advanced features and provide in-depth guidance, including tools and strategies particularly valuable for businesses.

Getting Acquainted with Snapchat

Upon opening the Snapchat app, you will be greeted by the camera view, which may be either facing you or pointing away, depending on your settings. To switch between these views, simply tap the smiley face icon surrounded by arrows located at the top right corner of your camera screen. This icon allows you to toggle between a selfie mode and capturing what's in front of you. It's easy to accidentally switch views, so don't be surprised if you find the camera facing you when you first log in.

Navigating Snapchat

Navigation within Snapchat primarily involves swiping gestures. Here's a brief guide to help you get acquainted with the interface:

- **Swipe Right:** This action will display your contacts list. Initially, this list may only include team members from Snapchat. To initiate a chat with any of your contacts, tap the speech bubble icon at the top right of the screen. For those with extensive contact lists, the magnifying glass icon can be used to search for specific individuals, streamlining the process of locating and interacting with them.

- **Swipe Left:** This gesture brings up the Stories page. Here, you will find stories from major brands and Snapchat partners featured prominently at the top. Stories from live events are listed under the 'Live' category. This section allows you to stay updated with real-time content and trends.

- **Swipe Down:** By swiping down from your home screen, you will access your Snapchat QR code, symbolized by the yellow icon with a ghost in the center. This QR code facilitates easy following; users can scan it to connect with you effortlessly. This innovative method simplifies the process of gaining followers and enhances user interaction.

Additional Features

On your home screen, you'll notice several additional features. For instance, your trophies and friend requests can be viewed, and you can manage your friends and add new contacts.

A gear icon located at the top right corner of the screen provides access to your personal settings. Tapping this icon will allow you to view and update your personal information. If you need to verify your account, you can enter the code sent to your mobile device here. Alternatively, if you have not provided a phone number, Snapchat may require you to solve a puzzle to confirm your identity.

This chapter has covered the essential aspects of navigating Snapchat. For a more comprehensive understanding, particularly of features that are highly beneficial for businesses, be sure to consult the upcoming chapters. They will offer detailed insights into the advanced functionalities and strategic uses of Snapchat for enhancing your brand's presence and engagement on the platform.

4

Snapchat Features that Businesses Use the Most

As highlighted in the previous chapter, this section will focus on key features that are particularly beneficial for businesses: the logo integration and QR code functionalities. While the previous chapter covered the basics of navigating Snapchat, this chapter will provide guidance on effectively utilizing your QR code and offer a workaround for the current limitation of not being able to upload your brand's logo directly to your profile.

Incorporating Your Logo and QR Code

Snapchat does not permit direct uploads of logos to profiles, so incorporating your brand's logo requires a creative approach. Snapchat allows users to take a series of five consecutive photos, which can be used to create a short GIF. You can utilize this feature by capturing a high-quality image of your logo. It's crucial to ensure that the camera remains perfectly still to maintain clarity. Alternatively, you can explore innovative ways to capture your logo in these five snapshots, which will be combined into a dynamic GIF format.

Regarding the QR code, it is designed for real-world interaction, allowing users to scan it to connect with you on Snapchat. Integrating your logo into this QR code can enhance brand recognition, but it must be done carefully to avoid disrupting the code's functionality. The QR code contains embedded data that Snapchat uses to recognize and link to your profile, so altering the design could impact its effectiveness.

Here's how you can integrate your logo into your QR code:

1.   **Download Your QR Code:** Access the Snapchat website, log in to your account, and download your QR code.

2.   **Edit Your QR Code:** For precise editing, use a program like Photoshop, which is ideal due to its layering capabilities. Begin by removing the white ghost icon from the code, and then place your logo on a new layer beneath the transparency of the ghost. If you prefer not to use Photoshop, consider hiring a professional from platforms like Fiverr to handle this task. Ensure that you provide the following guidelines to maintain the QR code's functionality:

   ◦ **Preserve the Ghost Shape:** Do not alter or remove the black border around the ghost icon, as this could render your QR code non-functional.

- **Avoid Stretching:** Maintain the original dimensions of the QR code; do not stretch or change its shape.
- **Color Integrity:** Do not invert or change the colors of the QR code.
- **Printing Considerations:** Avoid printing on glossy paper or cardstock, as the shine might interfere with scanning.

Once your QR code is ready, you can display it across various platforms—on your website, social media profiles, and physical locations. Consider showcasing it in high-visibility areas such as the walls of your physical stores, on business cards, or even on billboards and company vehicles. However, be sure to test the code's scannability in these contexts before committing significant resources.

In future chapters, specifically Chapters Six and Eight, we will explore additional Snapchat features beneficial for businesses, such as the Stories function, providing further insights into how to maximize your brand's presence on the platform.

5 |

Advanced Features of Snapchat

In this chapter, we will explore some of Snapchat's more advanced features. While we will touch on basic functionalities like video and photo features now, more in-depth topics, such as Snapchat Stories, will be addressed in subsequent chapters. Our goal here is to provide you with a solid foundation to effectively utilize these fundamental aspects of the platform.

Mastering Zoom in Your Videos

Snapchat allows for dynamic video capture beyond the default settings. Initially, your video will appear zoomed out. To zoom in, use a pinching gesture—place two fingers on the screen and spread them apart, much like zooming in on a web-page. Conversely, to zoom out, bring your fingers together. Additionally, if you wish to switch between the front and rear cameras, locate the camera toggle icon positioned at the top right of your video screen.

Utilizing Your Own Photos

You can enhance your one-on-one communications by incorporating photos from your phone's library. To do this, swipe right on the friend you wish to send a photo to and tap the blue bubble that appears. This action will open a private chat where you can tap the yellow circle, as if preparing to take a photo. In the camera view, look to the bottom right corner where you will find the last photo you took. Tap this photo to open your library, select the image you wish to share, and send it as a snap.

Enhancing Your Snaps and Videos

Adding captions to your snaps and videos is a common practice, but you can take it further to create visually appealing content. When you first add a caption, the app might prompt you to do so. If not, you can manually add text by tapping the

'T' icon at the top of the screen. For more emphasis, tap the 'T' icon again to enlarge and bold the text. You can adjust the size further by spreading your fingers apart on the text. This allows you to resize and reposition your text creatively.

In addition to text, Snapchat offers various creative tools. The paper icon to the left of the text icon provides access to a wide array of emojis. You can select an emoji, resize it, move it, and rotate it as needed. The pencil or pen icon on the right allows you to draw directly on your snap using a chosen color, which can be done with your finger or a stylus.

Another feature is the ability to enable geofilters. Go to your settings menu, select "Additional Services," and tap "Manage" to activate filters. Once enabled, you can swipe right on your photo to explore filters available based on your geographic location. Snapchat uses your ZIP code to offer region-specific filters, so take some time to explore and find those that best fit your content.

Additional Tips

Lastly, there are some advanced features worth noting. For instance, you can highlight individual words in your captions. Tap on a word to underline it, then press and hold to change its color. This feature can be used creatively, such as framing your photo with large letters. Experiment with different styles to see what best suits your needs.

Additionally, Snapchat allows you to replay a snap once per day. This option is available for the last snap you viewed, and the replay option will appear on your screen after the snap has expired.

With these features in mind, you can begin to craft engaging and visually appealing content on Snapchat. Future chapters will delve into more advanced tools and strategies, including the use of Stories, to further enhance your presence on the platform.

6

Introduction to Marketing on Snapchat

Marketing on Snapchat presents a unique opportunity, largely revolving around the platform's Stories feature. While the specifics of crafting Stories will be explored in Chapter 8, this chapter will focus on how to effectively utilize Stories for marketing purposes.

To begin, it's essential to understand what a Story is within the Snapchat ecosystem. For context, a "Snap" is a single video or image sent directly to a specific person. While Snaps can be used for marketing, their limited reach —being viewable by only one recipient at a time and disappearing within ten seconds—makes them less effective for broader marketing strategies. Therefore, we will concentrate on Stories, which offer more substantial marketing potential.

Stories differ significantly from Snaps. Unlike Snaps, which are fleeting, Stories comprise a series of images and videos that remain visible for 24 hours. Additionally, while Snaps are typically sent to individuals on your friends list or, in rare cases, to anyone who allows open Snaps, Stories can be set to be viewable by anyone you choose. This flexibility in visibility makes Stories a powerful tool for marketing, as they can be shared and thus reach a wider audience.

Configuring Your Account for Maximum Visibility

To ensure that your Stories are accessible to the broadest audience, you need to adjust your privacy settings. Start by opening Snapchat and swiping down to access the settings menu. Click on the gear icon located at the top right corner. From there, navigate to the settings for managing who can send you Snaps and who can view your Stories.

Adjust these settings to allow anyone to view your Stories if you aim to maximize your reach.

With these settings in place, you are ready to begin sharing Stories on Snapchat. Although we will cover the specifics of creating compelling Stories in Chapter 8, it's important to leverage this feature strategically. Promote your Stories across other social media platforms to drive traffic to your Snapchat content. By doing so, you can increase visibility and engagement with your Stories, particularly if they highlight products or services.

Remember, the key to effective storytelling on Snapchat lies in creating engaging and entertaining content. The goal is to captivate your audience so they are motivated to share your Stories with others and return for future updates. By maintaining high-quality, entertaining content, you ensure that your Stories are not only seen but eagerly anticipated by your audience.

7

Tips to get Your Initial Following

To achieve success in marketing on Snapchat, building a substantial following is essential. Just as with Twitter and Facebook, the more followers you have, the greater the likelihood that new users will be drawn to your content. This chapter will provide guidance on attracting your initial followers and highlight some practices to avoid.

Unleash Your Creativity

The foundation of engaging Snapchat content is creativity. Ensure that your posts are vibrant, imaginative, and showcase your unique artistic flair. Generic content, repetitive text, and dull product videos are unlikely to capture attention. Instead, focus on sharing dynamic images and videos of your product being used in innovative ways. Accompany these with lively captions and emojis to spark interest and encourage sharing.

Leverage Your Existing Social Networks

As mentioned previously, integrating your Snapchat presence with other social media platforms is crucial. To effectively drive followers to your Snapchat account, create enticing posts on platforms like Twitter, Facebook, and Instagram. Share exclusive teasers, such as promo codes or special offers available only through Snapchat. This strategy not only attracts your existing audience but also directs them to your Snapchat profile.

Promote Your Snapcode

Maximize the visibility of your Snapcode by placing it strategically across various channels. Display it prominently on your website, in-store signage, and other relevant locations where potential followers are likely to see it. Include the Snapcode on your business cards, in email signatures, and consider advertising on industry-specific forums.

The goal is to make it as easy as possible for people to discover and follow you on Snapchat.

Collaborate with Social Media Influencers

Engaging with influencers who have a significant online following can be a powerful way to increase your Snapchat audience. Identify YouTubers or other content creators who align with your brand and may have an interest in your products or services. Offering them exclusive deals or collaborations can encourage them to share your Snapchat profile with their followers, thereby expanding your reach.

Avoid Ineffective Strategies

To build a genuine and engaged following, steer clear of certain pitfalls. Avoid using services from platforms like Fiverr that promise a large number of followers, as these often involve fake accounts or bots that do not contribute to meaningful engagement. Such practices can also risk your account being banned. Additionally, ensure that your presence on Snapchat is personable and engaging. Users prefer to connect with a real, approachable individual rather than a faceless entity. Strive to maintain authenticity and accessibility in your interactions to foster a more vibrant and interactive community.

8

Want to Build Fans through Snapchat Stories?

When it comes to leveraging Snapchat for marketing, stories are more than just a tool for showcasing your products or services—they're an opportunity to captivate and engage your audience. Think of a Snapchat story as akin to a viral video; it's crucial that it's not overly promotional. Instead, aim for creativity, uniqueness, and emotional resonance. Your goal should be to craft content that intrigues and delights viewers, prompting them to share it with their friends. This not only boosts your visibility but also encourages people to follow you. Each story you create should balance promoting your product or service with engaging and entertaining content.

Crafting Exceptional Snapchat Stories

To master the art of creating compelling Snapchat stories, start by examining some of the most successful examples available online. Numerous standout stories have been highlighted on platforms like Buzzfeed, Mashable, and other prominent media outlets. As you explore these stories, think about what made them effective and entertaining. Consider how you might adapt similar creative strategies to your own Snapchat account, ensuring that your content is both engaging and subtly promotes your brand.

Remember, stories on Snapchat are not limited to static photos; they can also incorporate dynamic videos. Pairing videos with images can enhance the storytelling experience. The foundation of a great story is a creative idea. Gather your team, friends, or colleagues and brainstorm innovative concepts. Draw inspiration from a variety of sources: conduct a Google search for random keywords, explore images related to those words, or observe your surroundings for amusing elements. Reflect on recent content that made you laugh and analyze why it resonated with you. There are countless ways to generate inspiring story ideas.

Once you have a concept, storyboard your story. This involves planning the sequence of your snaps and videos to ensure a cohesive and engaging narrative. Carefully map out the order in which your content will appear, keeping in mind that a well-structured story will maintain viewers' interest and encourage them to keep swiping. Aim for brevity; much like YouTube videos, Snapchat stories should be concise to avoid losing viewer engagement. Typically, stories that are just a few minutes long are most effective in keeping the audience's attention.

With these strategies in mind, you're ready to start creating captivating stories on Snapchat. Approach each story with creativity and a clear vision, and watch as your brand garners attention and followers through engaging and memorable content.

9

Discover Snapchat's Partner Program

One aspect of Snapchat's advertising opportunities that might pique your interest is their exclusive partner program known as Discover. This program, while highly sought after, is generally accessible only to major brands due to its substantial cost of $750,000 per day. However, there are alternative avenues for gaining visibility on Discover, which can be more attainable for brands with smaller budgets.

Notably, some of the prominent brands that have secured spots on Discover are offering opportunities for other brands to advertise within their Discover space. This arrangement allows the major brands to recoup a portion of their substantial investment, while providing smaller brands with the chance to gain significant exposure at a more affordable rate. If you have a budget of around $50,000, this could be an excellent opportunity to achieve high visibility on the platform.

For smaller brands or businesses, current options for Snapchat advertising are limited. At present, Snapchat does not offer an advertising model akin to Facebook's for smaller enterprises. There would need to be significant changes to the platform to allow advertising within snaps, videos, and other areas of the site. While this possibility could arise in the future, Snapchat's advertising landscape remains primarily dominated by high-budget Discover placements.

In summary, if you have considerable funds allocated for advertising, Snapchat's Discover program or its associated advertising opportunities could be highly beneficial for you. For smaller businesses or those seeking more cost-effective marketing strategies, it is advisable to utilize the marketing techniques outlined in this book. These strategies, tailored to the current capabilities of Snapchat, can still provide valuable engagement and visibility without the need for substantial investment in Discover.

10

Viewing Statistics

When utilizing Snapchat for your marketing efforts, it is essential to understand and leverage the available statistics to enhance your brand's performance. Although Snapchat does not provide comprehensive analytics on visitor details for your story page, it does offer several useful metrics that can help you gauge the effectiveness of your content. In this discussion, we will explore these metrics and introduce some emerging alternatives that might offer the detailed analytics you need.

Snapchat provides a few key statistics, primarily focused on your stories— the main feature relevant for marketing purposes. Here's a closer look at the metrics available:

1.   **Total Unique Views**: This metric indicates how many distinct users have opened your story and viewed at least the first frame. While this doesn't account for users who may not have continued past the initial frame, it gives a solid understanding of the reach of your story. To access this data, simply check the number of views on the first frame of your story.

2.   **Total Story Completions**: To determine how many viewers completed your story, refer to the last frame of your story. This count reflects how many users watched through to the end. Remember to monitor these figures after your story has been live for the full 24 hours.

3.   **Completion Rate**: This is a crucial metric that provides insight into the effective-

ness of your story. Calculate your completion rate by comparing the total unique views to the total story completions. For instance, if 1,000 people start watching your story but only 450 finish it, your completion rate would be 45%. A higher completion rate signifies a more engaging story.

4. **Stopping Point**: Analyze the point at which viewers tend to stop watching your story. Identifying a pattern in these stopping points can help you pinpoint sections of your story that may need improvement. It's important to note that the issue might lie in the content leading up to the stopping point, not necessarily the exact frame where viewers lost interest.

In addition to Snapchat's built-in analytics, there are several third-party companies that now offer detailed analytics services for Snapchat. These companies have emerged recently, providing innovative solutions and garnering positive feedback from businesses seeking to optimize their Snapchat marketing strategies. When selecting an analytics provider, ensure you research their reputation and verify that their pricing aligns with industry standards. Investing in these tools can provide you with the deeper insights needed to refine your content and make informed decisions about your Snapchat marketing approach.

11

Using Snapchat at Live Events to get Followers

In this chapter, we will explore effective strategies for leveraging live events to attract followers to your Snapchat account. To start, open your Snapchat app and navigate to the Discover page. Here, you will notice a section labeled "Live" and a series of stories listed below. It's important to differentiate this from Snapchat's "Our Story" feature, which curates snaps and videos from various live events into a single story accessible to all users, regardless of their following.

For the purposes of this discussion, we are focusing on using Snapchat to promote and enhance live events organized by your company. These are events where attendees can physically participate, and Snapchat can play a key role in both drawing people to the event and encouraging those who are already present to follow your account.

To attract attendees from Snapchat to your live event, start by crafting an engaging story that generates excitement and interest. Begin by posting teasers about the event at least 24 hours prior to its start. This will give potential attendees ample time to plan their visit. As the event unfolds, create and share a new story that provides live updates, images, and videos from the event itself, allowing your audience to experience the excitement in real-time.

This approach not only helps in attracting individuals who need time to prepare for the event but also appeals to those who are more spontaneous and may decide to attend at the last minute. It is essential to remember that this strategy is most effective if you have a significant number of followers in the same city where the event is taking place. Large brands in major cities typically have no issue with this, as do small businesses with local brick-and-mortar stores. However, businesses that operate solely online and have a small following may face challenges in generating substantial attendance if their followers are not located nearby.

To maximize engagement, consider incorporating promotions, special offers, or giveaways in your Snapchat stories. This added incentive can significantly increase both the number of attendees and the number of new followers who engage with your Snapchat account. Whether you're encouraging local followers to join the event or enticing new followers to check out your content, these strategies will help you leverage Snapchat effectively for your live event marketing.

12

Delivering Personal Content through Snapchat

This chapter aims to provide you with insightful strategies for delivering personalized content to your Snapchat followers. We will delve into the types of content you can share, offer creative ideas for personal engagements, and provide essential tips for effective delivery. The focus here is on establishing a direct connection with your followers through tailored interactions, which can significantly enhance your promotional efforts.

One effective strategy involves integrating personal content with your ongoing promotions. For example, imagine you've announced on your website that you will be giving away a limited number of free items or gift certificates. To qualify for this giveaway, recipients must be followers on Snapchat and receive a personalized snap from you. To optimize this approach, select a specific day and time window within that week for the giveaway. During this period, amplify your promotional activities to capture the attention of your Snapchat followers. Knowing that your audience is eager for the giveaway will encourage them to engage more actively with your stories and updates.

Another innovative way to utilize personal content is by expressing gratitude to customers who make a purchase on your website. By requesting their Snapchat ID on the order form, you can send personalized thank-you snaps. Following this, you can create a compelling story featuring these thank-you messages. This not only fosters a stronger connection with your customers but also showcases your appreciation for their support, enhancing their overall experience with your brand.

Additionally, consider leveraging personal communication to drive referrals and expand your follower base. Encourage your existing followers to refer new users by offering them a significant discount or a free item in exchange for bringing in a certain number of new followers. To facilitate this process, you might ask them to share their referral activity on another social media platform, such as Twitter. Provide a specific hashtag and instruct them to post the Snapchat ID of the new follower along with the hashtag. This way, you can monitor your Snapchat follower list to confirm the new additions and grant credit to the referrer.

In summary, personal communication on Snapchat offers various avenues to boost engagement and grow your business. By thoughtfully integrating personal touches into your promotional strategies, expressing appreciation to customers, and encouraging referrals, you can create meaningful interactions that enhance your brand's visibility and foster a loyal following.

13

Give Followers an Inside Look

Another effective strategy for leveraging Snapchat is to offer your followers an exclusive behind-the-scenes look into your operations or projects. This approach provides several advantages. Firstly, it keeps your brand top-of-mind for your Snapchat audience, ensuring that they think of you when they require your product or service. Secondly, if the behind-the-scenes content is engaging and your ongoing activities are intriguing, it will encourage your followers to share your snaps, increasing your reach.

To maximize this strategy, ensure that all your other social media platforms are aware that you're sharing exclusive behind-the-scenes content on Snapchat. Promote your Snapchat account on platforms like Facebook, Twitter, and Instagram to attract followers from those channels who are eager to access your unique content. This cross-promotion can effectively increase your Snapchat follower count.

Additionally, use Snapchat to drive traffic to your website. Incorporate links and compelling calls-to-action within your Snapchat stories to guide viewers to your site. Offer clear incentives for them to visit, such as exclusive content, special offers, or valuable information. By doing so, you not only enhance engagement on Snapchat but also direct traffic to your website where you can capture leads or sales.

For long-term benefits, consider encouraging your Snapchat followers to sign up for your mailing list. Emails typically have a longer engagement time compared to social media posts or snaps, providing you with a more stable channel for communication and marketing.

Ultimately, the key to success with Snapchat is consistent interaction with your audience. Whenever you have noteworthy behind-the-scenes content or other valuable updates, share them on Snapchat. Always seize opportunities to provide your followers with exclusive insights or content that they can't find elsewhere. Ensure that your calls-to-action are coupled with tangible benefits to motivate followers to take the desired actions.

14

How to Run Contests & Promotions on Snapchat?

Snapchat provides an excellent platform for running contests and promotions, offering businesses a unique opportunity to express gratitude and boost engagement through exciting initiatives. Many brands on Snapchat leverage this strategy to thank their followers, often with special discounts, while simultaneously increasing their follower base. In this chapter, we'll delve into effective methods for crafting successful contests and promotions on Snapchat, and explore the benefits they can offer.

Designing Your Promotion

The first step in executing a successful Snapchat promotion is designing it thoughtfully. Consider the nature of the contest or promotion and determine what actions you will require from your participants. For instance, you might ask followers to add you as a friend on Snapchat and then submit a video or snapshot related to a specific theme. Careful planning of these logistics is crucial to ensure a smooth and engaging experience for your participants.

Promoting Your Promotion

Once your promotion is designed, it's time to spread the word. Promote your contest across various channels, including your physical store, website, and other social media platforms. It's important to clearly communicate the details of the contest to your audience. Additionally, inform them that any content they create and submit may be used in future promotions. This transparency will help manage expectations and encourage more participation.

Managing Contest Entries

After launching your promotion, efficiently manage and review the entries. For example, if participants are submitting videos, use a reliable third-party tool to collect and save these entries, as Snapchat's ephemeral nature means that videos and snaps disappear within seconds or 24 hours, depending on their format. Utilizing such tools ensures that you don't miss any submissions and can properly review all entries.

Selecting Winners and Following Up

The final step is to determine the winners of your promotion or decide on how to distribute rewards, whether through individual prizes or promotional codes for all participants. Your approach can vary based on your promotional goals and the nature of the contest. A well-executed promotion not only generates excitement but also increases the likelihood that participants will continue engaging with your Snapchat content, including your snaps, videos, and stories.

By running a well-planned and executed contest or promotion, you'll foster greater interaction with your followers and enhance your overall presence on Snapchat.

15

Aligning Yourself with Niche Influencers on Snapc

Exploring marketing strategies for your company on Snapchat can lead you to consider the powerful tool of niche influencers. This method, widely used by major brands, involves partnering with influential figures within a specific niche to promote your products or services. For instance, cosmetic companies often collaborate with renowned makeup tutorial creators on YouTube, capitalizing on their established audiences to enhance brand visibility. This approach can be highly effective for your marketing strategy on Snapchat as well.

Understanding Niche Influencers

Niche influencers are individuals who wield significant influence within a specific industry or interest area. They have cultivated a large and engaged following that trusts their recommendations. When these influencers endorse products or services, their followers are likely to make purchases based on these endorsements. This trust and reach are why brands frequently provide influencers with free samples and collaborate with them to promote their offerings.

Benefits of Partnering with Niche Influencers

Utilizing niche influencers offers several advantages. Firstly, you gain access to their dedicated audience, potentially converting their followers into customers for your own brand. This exposure can also elevate your company's name within industry-specific circles, enhancing your reputation and reach. Engaging with influencers helps position your brand as a trusted choice among their established follower base.

Effective Strategies for Using Niche Influencers

There are various creative ways to collaborate with niche influencers. One common method is sending them free samples of your products or services, provided they align with your industry. Alternatively, you might allow an influencer to take over your Snapchat account for a day, providing fresh content and engaging directly with your audience. This approach has gained popularity and can offer a unique, personal touch to your marketing efforts.

Finding the Right Niche Influencers

Identifying the right niche influencers for your industry is relatively straightforward. Utilize platforms like Klout, PeerIndex, and Cred to measure influence and find potential partners. Additionally, explore social media platforms such as Twitter, Instagram, Pinterest, and Facebook to discover individuals with substantial followings in your field. Don't overlook Snapchat itself, as it may also host influential figures within your niche who can amplify your brand's presence.

By effectively leveraging niche influencers, you can enhance your brand's visibility, build trust with new audiences, and create meaningful connections within your industry.

16

Measuring Your Success with Snapchat

Assessing the success of your Snapchat marketing efforts involves more than simply tallying numbers. To gauge whether your campaign was effective, you need to employ creative methods for evaluating both quantitative and qualitative aspects of your results. While numerical data provides a crucial baseline, understanding the broader impact and reception of your campaign is equally important.

First, Let's Address the Numbers

Quantitative data is fundamental to measuring success. To effectively evaluate your Snapchat campaign, track how many individuals you reached and how many of those engaged with your call to action—whether that involved signing up for an email list, using a specific hashtag on Twitter, or taking another desired action. Utilize the analytics tools available on Snapchat, as discussed in the relevant chapter, alongside any additional methods you have for tracking responses. This will give you a clear picture of your campaign's reach and effectiveness.

Next, Consider the Demographics

Demographic information is critical for understanding who engaged with your campaign. By analyzing this data, you can determine which segments of your audience were most responsive to your marketing efforts, allowing you to refine and target future campaigns more effectively. Acquiring demographic insights can be challenging, so it may be beneficial to consult with analytics companies, as mentioned previously, to obtain detailed demographic profiles that your own efforts might not reveal.

Finally, Evaluate User Response

Beyond numbers and demographics, it's essential to gauge user sentiment regarding your campaign. Understanding how users felt about your marketing efforts—whether they found the offer compelling or were hesitant—provides valuable feedback. This qualitative insight can significantly inform and enhance your future campaigns. Conduct surveys, engage with your audience through follow-up messages, or analyze user comments and reactions to better understand their perceptions and experiences.

By combining numerical data, demographic insights, and user feedback, you can obtain a comprehensive view of your Snapchat campaign's success and identify areas for improvement. This multifaceted approach will enable you to refine your strategies and achieve more impactful results in future marketing endeavors.

17

Learning From Other Brands on Snapchat

Learning from other brands on Snapchat is a strategic approach that can greatly enhance your own marketing efforts. Given that Snapchat is a dynamic platform with ever-evolving trends and marketing ideas, staying abreast of the latest strategies employed by other companies can be time-consuming but invaluable. To optimize your approach, focus on observing and analyzing the strategies of major brands, as these examples are often more accessible and can offer valuable insights. In this chapter, we will explore effective methods for discovering what successful brands are doing on Snapchat and how you can adapt their strategies to benefit your own brand.

News Articles

Keeping up with marketing news is an excellent way to uncover insights about Snapchat's latest trends and successful strategies employed by leading brands. With Snapchat's significant user base and its recent decision to decline Facebook's acquisition offer, the platform is frequently covered in industry news. Regularly check marketing news websites and set up alerts for Snapchat-related topics to stay informed about innovative campaigns and successful tactics used by major brands.

Consult Industry Peers

Engaging with professionals in your industry can provide a wealth of information and fresh perspectives. Networking with others who share your market focus allows for the exchange of valuable insights and strategies. These conversations can reveal effective methods and creative approaches that you might not have discovered on your own. While direct competitors might be more reserved, most professionals within your industry are likely to be open to sharing their experiences and discussing their Snapchat strategies.

Follow Marketing Blogs and Trend Analysts

Subscribing to reputable marketing blogs and trend analysts is another effective way to stay updated on Snapchat strategies. Many marketing bloggers conduct in-depth research and provide timely updates on emerging trends and successful campaigns. Set up regular updates or RSS feeds from these sources to receive the latest information directly. Utilize Google search to find blogs and analysts who specialize in Snapchat marketing to ensure you are accessing the most relevant and current insights.

By leveraging these strategies, you can gain valuable knowledge from successful brands, enhance your Snapchat marketing efforts, and stay ahead in the ever-evolving landscape of digital marketing.

18

Integrating Snapchat with Your Site & Social Media

Integrating Snapchat with your website and social media can vary in complexity depending on the platform you are using for your site. With numerous website creation tools and content management systems available today, the ease of integration can differ significantly. In this chapter, we will explore how to seamlessly incorporate Snapchat into both your website and your social media profiles, providing you with practical tips and strategies.

Integrating Snapchat with Your Website

For those using WordPress as their content management system, the process of integrating Snapchat will largely depend on your chosen theme. While most WordPress themes offer built-in options for linking to popular social media platforms like Facebook, Twitter, and Pinterest, Snapchat integration may not be as straightforward. However, you can still incorporate your Snapchat presence by using a text widget to display your Snapchat ID and QR code. Placing these elements in a prominent location, such as the sidebar of your WordPress site, ensures that visitors can easily find and connect with you on Snapchat.

If your website is custom-built using HTML, you may need to collaborate with your web designer to create dedicated space for your Snapchat QR code and other relevant information. Ideally, the QR code should be placed in a highly visible area, such as the header of your homepage. This strategic placement allows visitors to quickly scan the code and follow you on Snapchat, enhancing your overall engagement.

Integrating Snapchat with Social Media

Integrating Snapchat with your social media profiles requires a more nuanced approach, given the limitations and policies of various platforms. For example, Twitter does not offer a dedicated space for posting QR codes or Snapchat information. While you might consider updating your profile picture with your Snapchat QR code, this approach could be problematic. Both Twitter and Snapchat may not support or appreciate the use of a competing platform's QR code, and it could detract from the quality and clarity of your profile picture.

A more subtle method is to incorporate your Snapchat QR code into the background elements of your social media profiles. On Twitter, this means placing the QR code in the background area of your tweets, while on Facebook, you can include it in the header profile area. Ensure that the QR code is not overly intrusive, as maintaining a professional and visually appealing profile is essential.

Additionally, consistently remind your social media followers about your Snapchat presence through regular updates and posts. By integrating your Snapchat details into your social media feeds and leveraging background elements creatively, you can effectively drive traffic to your Snapchat account while adhering to the guidelines of each platform.

In summary, integrating Snapchat with your website and social media requires a thoughtful approach tailored to the specific tools and platforms you are using. By strategically placing QR codes and providing clear reminders, you can enhance your Snapchat presence and encourage greater engagement from your audience.

Conclusion

Snapchat has become one of the most captivating social media platforms in recent times, offering a distinctive mode of communication through visuals and short videos. Its novel format presents an engaging way for users to interact, and it's intriguing to watch the platform's ongoing evolution. Recognizing Snapchat's potential, an increasing number of businesses are dedicating a considerable part of their marketing budgets to connect with its vibrant user base.

This book delves into the various facets of utilizing Snapchat for marketing purposes. It starts with the benefits of engaging with this platform and walks you through setting up an account to effectively establish your online presence. It also outlines the process for creating your QR code, which can be employed across various channels such as your website, brick-and-mortar locations, business cards, and other social media profiles.

Key subjects addressed include crafting captivating Snapchat stories and tactics for amassing an initial following. The book offers comprehensive insights into Snapchat's analytics tools to monitor and assess your marketing campaigns, with advice on how to interpret these metrics for measuring success. It further examines the integration of Snapchat with other social networks and the use of live events to heighten user engagement. The strategy of collaborating with niche influencers to broaden your audience is also presented.

The aim of this book is to provide you with the expertise and resources to confidently utilize Snapchat and fully leverage its capabilities. Although marketing success on Snapchat is not assured, the trend of businesses significantly investing in the platform is a testament to its potential. With numerous companies experiencing considerable success and dedicating large budgets—sometimes up to three-quarters of a million dollars per day—to Snapchat advertising, there lies a substantial opportunity for you to attain similar achievements.